AF264409

I AM.

·Ana

Published by: Kindle Direct Publishing

ISBN: 978-1-0691139-0-0 (softcover)

I AM.

I AM. is about a country as old as the first civilizations. Its geographic position as a crossroads connecting the Mediterranean Sea with Asia, Lebanon is unique in its multiculturalism.

Throughout its history, Lebanon has come under foreign rule, including Babylonians, Persians, Greeks, and Romans.
Despite foreign domination, Lebanon's mountainous areas have provided it citizens with protection against threats, enabling survival of the countries identity.

Lebanon holds top rank as sea bearing commerce exporter and importer, introducing trading goods to countries in the East.

.Ana

أنا أكون. يدور حول بلد قديم قدم الحضارات الأولى. موقعه الجغرافي كمفترق طرق يربط البحر الأبيض المتوسط مع آسيا، لبنان فريد من نوعه في تعدد الثقافات.

طوال تاريخه، خضع لبنان للحكم الأجنبي، بما في ذلك البابليون والفرس واليونانيين والرومان.
على الرغم من الهيمنة الأجنبية، وفّرت المناطق الجبلية في لبنان لمواطنيها الحماية من التهديدات، مما مكّن من بقاء هوية البلد.

يحتل لبنان المرتبة الأولى كمصدر ومستورد للتجارة البحرية، حيث يقدم السلع التجارية إلى دول الشرق.

Contents

Contents

Contents

LAUGHTER.

.Dhikrayat

LAUGHTER.

old dwellings holds
countless memories of
laughter and love.

.Dhikrayat

المساكن القديمة تحمل ذكريات لا
تعد ولا تحصى من الضحك والحب.

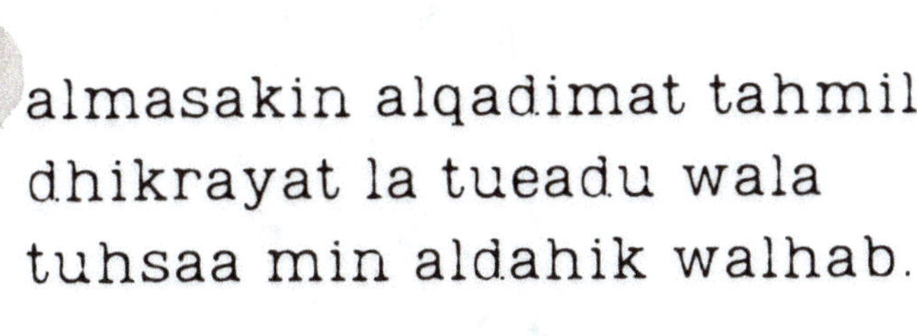

almasakin alqadimat tahmil
dhikrayat la tueadu wala
tuhsaa min aldahik walhab.

OF
HOPE.

Al' Amal

love and hope hold an
inherent value that
cannot be measured.

OF
HOPE.

alhubu wal'amal lahuma
qimat muta'asilat la
yumkin qiasuha.

الحب والأمل لهما قيمة متأصلة لا
يمكن قياسها.

.Al' Amal

LIFE.

.Hayet

LIFE.

all life is important. why is
mine any less special?

.Hayet

الحياة كلها مهمة. لماذا هو أقل خصوصية؟

alhayat kuluha muhimatun. limadha
hu 'aqalu khususiatin?

LABNEH.

.Lebnah

sweet like labneh, and comforting.
welcoming all with opened arms.

LABNEH.

hulwat mithl allabanat
wamurihati. altarhib bialjamie
bi'adhrue maftuhatin.

حلوة مثل اللبنة ومريحة. الترحيب بالجميع
بأذرع مفتوحة.

PEARL.

.LuLu

PEARL.

shining, shimmering, splendid as
the sea, the pearl is the eye of the
country.

.Lulu

mushriqatu, mutla'aliati, rayieat
kalbahra, alluwluat hi eayn
albaladi.

مشرقة، متلألئة، رائعة كالبحر، اللؤلؤة هي عين
البلاد.

THYME.

Za'atar

THYME.

a fragrant blend of toasted
sesame, i am a part of
origin history.

Za'atar

mazij eitriun min alsimsim
almuhamas, 'ana juz' min tarikh
almansha.

مزيج عطري من السمسم المحمص، أنا جزء من تاريخ
المنشأ.

LIBERTY.

.Al' Huriya

freedom and liberty to everyone, i
am a country that is French,
Roman and Lebanese blood.

LIBERTY.

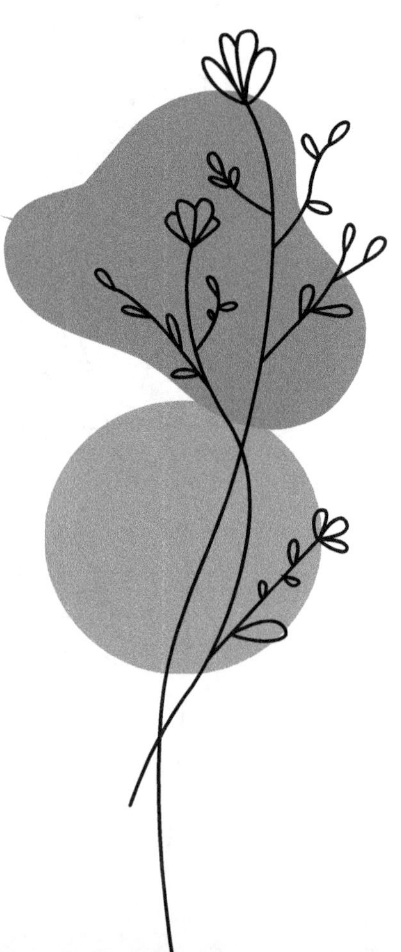

alhuriyat walhuriyat liljamiei, 'ana
balad dhu dima' faransiat warumaniat
walubnaniatin.

الحرية والحرية للجميع، أنا بلد ذو دماء فرنسية ورومانية
ولبنانية.

CLIVE.

Zaytoun

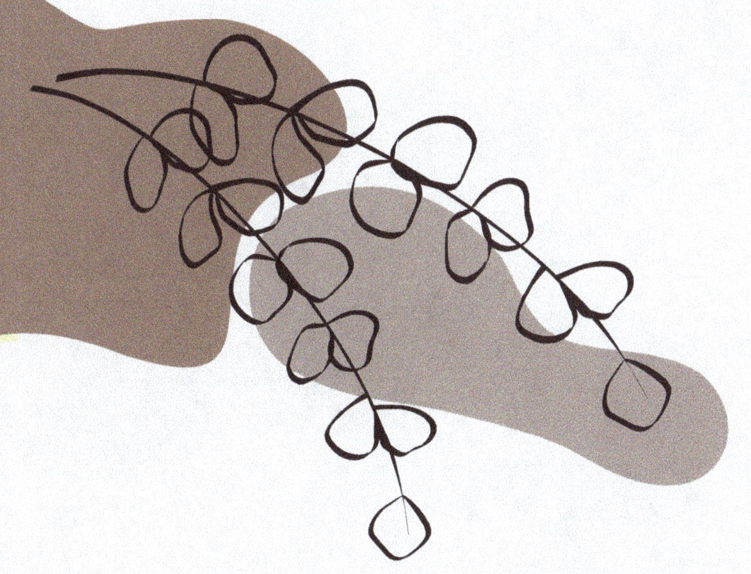

OLIVE.

just as the olive is versatile, the
Lebanese race will withstand anything.
becoming stronger as one.

fakama 'ana alzaytun mutaeadid
alaistiemalati, faljins allubnaniu
sayasmud 'amam 'ayi shay'in. tusbih
'aqwaa kawahidi.

فكما أن الزيتون متعدد الاستعمالات، فالجنس اللبناني
سيصمد أمام أي شيء. تصبح أقوى كواحد.

FLAG.

FLAG.

red, white, green. the flag represents
bloodshed, purity, and peace.

al'ahmar wal'abyad wal'akhdari.
yumathil aleilm safk aldima' walnaqa'
walsalami.

الأحمر والأبيض والأخضر. يمثل العلم سفك الدماء
والنقاء والسلام.

LANGUAGES.

.Al' Lughat

LANGUAGES.

the Phoenicians, we introduced the alphabet, English and French to the world.

alfiniqiuwna, 'adkhalna alhuruf
al'abjadiat wal'iinjiliziat walfaransiat
'iilaa alealami.

الفينيقيون، أدخلنا الحروف الأبجدية والإنجليزية
والفرنسية إلى العالم.

GARDEN.

.Al' Haqli

filled with mulberry, blackberries and a
variety of fruits. all are welcome at
grandpa's garden.

GARDEN.

maliyat bialtuwt waltuwt al'aswad
wamajmueatan mutanawieatan min
alfawakihi. aljamie murahab bihim fi
hadiqat aljid.

مليئة بالتوت والتوت الأسود ومجموعة متنوعة من
الفواكه. الجميع مرحب بهم في حديقة الجد.

JOY.

.Farah

joy, happiness, delight, the intelligence
of the country is found in the happiness
of the people.

JOY.

alfarah, alsaeadatu, albahjatu, dhaka'
alwatan mawjud fi saeadat alnaasi.

الفرح، السعادة، البهجة، ذكاء الوطن موجود في سعادة الناس.

GOLD.

.Dhabab

the economic importance of banks in
Lebanon is as beneficial and sacred as
gold. taking it away means an emaciated
and debilitated country of poverty.

GOLD.

'iina al'ahamiyat alaiqtisadiat lilmasarif
fi lubnan mufidat wamuqadasat mithl
aldhahabi. 'inn 'akhdhaha beydan yaeni
dawlat alfaqr alhazilat walmunhikati.

إن الأهمية الاقتصادية للمصارف في لبنان مفيدة
ومقدسة مثل الذهب. إن أخذها بعيدًا يعني دولة الفقر
الهزيلة والمنهكة.

PRINCESS.

.Amira

PRINCESS.

refined beauty embodying grace and
nobility, representative of a person of
elegance and richness.

Amira

jamal raqi yujasid alniemat walnabla,
wayumathil shkhsan yatamatae
bial'anaqat walghinaa.

جمال راقي يجسد النعمة والنبل، ويمثل شخصًا يتمتع
بالأناقة والغنى.

PEACE.

Salam

PEACE.

ceasefire is what the country needs. to
reconcile amongst the darkness. the
strength and resilience of the people will
shine a light of hope in a country filled
with darkness.

waqf 'iitlaq alnaar hu ma tahtajuh
albaladi. liltasaluh bayn alzalam . 'iina
quat alshaeb wasumudah satudi' nur
al'amal fi balad yamlawuh alzalamu.

وقف إطلاق النار هو ما تحتاجه البلاد. للتصالح بين
الظلام . إن قوة الشعب وصموده ستضيء نور الأمل في
بلد يملؤه الظلام.

KUNAFA.

.Kanafeh

K U N A F A.

made with mozzarella cheese and pastry
layers, this dessert is as unique as
Lebanon. many sweet layers fill your
taste buds with warmth and happiness.

.Kanafeh

hadhih alhalwaa masnueat min jubnat
almuzarilaa watabaqat min almueajanati,
wahi faridat min naweiha mithl lubnan.
aleadid min altabaqat alhulwat tamla
dhawqak bialdif' walsaeadati.

هذه الحلوى مصنوعة من جبنة الموزاريلا وطبقات من
المعجنات، وهي فريدة من نوعها مثل لبنان. العديد من
الطبقات الحلوة تملأ ذوقك بالدفء والسعادة.

BAALBEK.

.Baalbek

BAALBEK.

Roman pillars take root in the ground
and reflect a history of ancient rule.

Baalbek

tatajadhar al'aemidat alruwmaniat fi
al'ard wataekis tarykhan min alhukm
alqadimi.

تتجذر الأعمدة الرومانية في الأرض وتعكس تاريخًا من
الحكم القديم.

JEITA GROTTO.

.Jeita

one of the wonders of the world, the
Jeita grotto has an important social and
cultural impact on Lebanon.

JEITA GROTTO.

tuetabar magharat jaeita 'iihdaa eajayib
aldunya, walaha tathir aijtimaeiun
wathaqafiun muhimun ealaa lubnan.

تعتبر مغارة جعيتا إحدى عجائب الدنيا، ولها تأثير
اجتماعي وثقافي مهم على لبنان.

PINECONE.

Alsanubar

named the "white gold", the pinecone is
high quality with a distinctive flavor
exclusive to the gold club.

PINECONE.

yutlq ealaa kuz alsanawbar asm
"aldhahab al'abyadu", wayatamayaz
bijawdat ealiat wanikhat mumayazat
hsryan linadi aldhahbi.

يُطلق على كوز الصنوبر اسم "الذهب الأبيض"، ويتميز
بجودة عالية ونكهة مميزة حصريًا لنادي الذهب.

Alsanubar

TUMERIC
CAKE.

Stout

TUMERIC CAKE.

light and fluffy, sfouf is a cake made
with golden powder, this sweet is as
delightful as the sun.

alsufuf khafif waraqiqu, wahu eibarat
ean kaekat masnueat min mashuq
dhahabi, wahadhih alhalwaa mubhijat
mithl alshamsi.

السفوف خفيف ورقيق، وهو عبارة عن كعكة مصنوعة
من مسحوق ذهبي، وهذه الحلوى مبهجة مثل الشمس.

FREEDOM.

.Huriya

FREEDOM.

to have freedom is something to never
take for granted.

.Huriya

'an tatamatae bialhuriyat hu 'amr la yajib 'an taetabirah amran mfrwghan minhu.

أن تتمتع بالحرية هو أمر لا يجب أن تعتبره أمرًا مفروغًا منه.

SWEETEST
KISS.

Basbousa

Egyptian in origin, basbousa is known as the sweetest kiss for its tender and flaky cake, bathed in a sweet syrup.

SWEETEST KISS.

tuerf albisbusatu, misriatan al'asla,
bi'anaha 'ahlaa qiblatan bisabab
kaekatiha alraqiqat walqashariat
almughataat bialsharab alhulu.

تُعرف البسبوسة، مصرية الأصل، بأنها أحلى قبلة
بسبب كعكتها الرقيقة والقشارية المغطاة بالشراب
الحلو.

PEACE.

Salam

demanding peace is not an option, peace
comes from confidence.

PEACE.

'iina almutalabat bialsalam laysat
khiara, falsalam yati min althiqati.

إن المطالبة بالسلام ليست خيارا، فالسلام يأتي من
الثقة.

Salam

LEBANON.

.Lubnan

a tremendous force of a surging power
brings forth a beauty of east and west
named Lebanon.

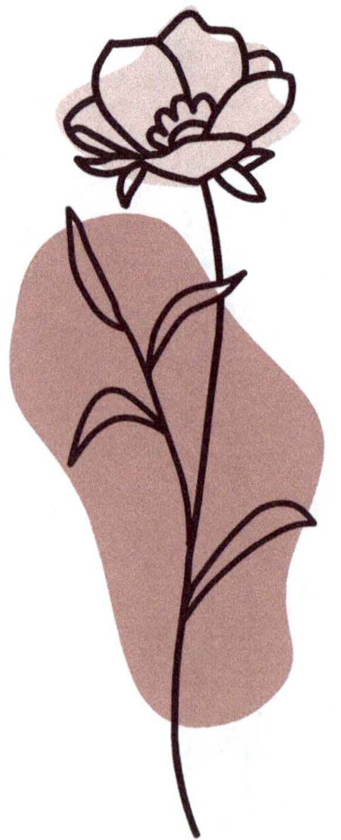

LEBANON.

quat hayilat min alquat almutasaeidat
tanbathiq jamal alsharq walgharb
aismuh lubnanu.

قوة هائلة من القوة المتصاعدة تنبثق جمال الشرق
والغرب اسمه لبنان.